Time Flies

JOURNAL

Time Flies

JOURNAL

A BIRD LOVER'S DAYBOOK

Willow Creek Press

Published by Willow Creek Press
P.O. Box 147, Minocqua, Wisconsin 54548

ISBN-10: 1-59543-421-6
ISBN-13: 978-1-59543-421-0

Printed in Canada

Time gives us special perspective. Looking one way it is easy to connect the dots of past events that lead to another event, such as a war, or a marriage. Looking the other way, dots that eventually will be connectable are impossible to discern in the clutter of possibilities.

—Louis Menand

Birds keep to their timeless ways and yet somehow stay in tune with changes man has wrought.

—John V. Dennis

The male Cardinal's tropical red seems misplaced in northern snows.
A three-day reserve of fat helps it outlast winter storms.

By one measure the cardinal is America's most popular bird. It represents more states than any other species—seven—including Ohio, Indiana, North Carolina, West Virginia, Virginia, Kentucky, and Illinois. (The Western Meadowlark follows with six.) Throughout its range, the cardinal is a homebody, spending its entire life within a mile or two of where it was born. Still, since Audubon first painted it, the cardinal has spread far to the north of its traditional Ohio River valley limit, following thickets along rivers, and perhaps establishing leapfrogged footholds after being freed from cages, where settlers kept them like canaries. Sunflowers from bird feeders have undoubtedly helped recent northward movements.

Today seems to prove the theory of relativity, which states that time is relative, not constant, in duration. Each year it seems that the last year flew by like the blur of hummingbird wings, but the year ahead seems to stretch forever. Maybe it won't hurt to squander a little time watching birds.

A noisy, excitable Carolina wren animates a snowman.

Several decades ago in one Midwestern city, an Audubon Christmas Bird Count tallied exactly 600 Carolina wrens. A couple of weeks after the count, a devastating blizzard struck. The next year the same Count registered just six wrens—a 99 percent decline. Wrens eventually made a nice come-back in the area, but have never regained pre-blizzard abundance.

Mechanical clocks did not exist until the 12th century, when Benedictine Monks developed them to help keep better track of devotional hours. In "The Cincinnati Arch, Learning from Nature in the City," John Tallmadge describes, "By the end of the 12th century, clock towers had sprung up in towns all over Europe. Business and government leaders were quick to recognize the clock's potential for organizing and controlling both people and work, thereby increasing productivity. The clock also allowed secular interests to siphon power away from the church. So the new device quickly became ubiquitous and indispensable, extending its dominion into every aspect of life until, in our day, mechanical time seems altogether natural, more familiar even than the movement of the sun, the moon, or the stars."

Round mound upon round mound; displaying a snowman's silhouette, a migrant snowy owl in the Midwest hunts from atop a hay bale on a winter dawn.

How many species of birds will you record this year? Before WWII, the highest official one-year count for North American species stood below 500. As transportation, communication, and equipment (including field guides) improved, so did birding. In 1952 the 500 barrier was broken for the first time, and in 1953 the man who "wrote the book" on bird identification, Roger Tory Peterson, again flew past that record with 572 species. In 1971, the legendary birder Ted Parker finally soared over the 600 ceiling. Now, some high-flying birders have seen more than 700 North American species in a year.

The late Phoebe Snetsinger has a place in the *Guinness Book of World Records* for her amazing lifetime bird list of 8,450 species from around the world.

Sir Isaac Newton speculated that the universe sits within a container of time, and time would exist whether the universe does or does not. Other philosophers and scientists have argued that time could not exist without the universe. They say time measures change, and without the universe there is no change, and thus no time.

American golden plovers spend winter 8,000 miles south of their tundra nesting grounds.

During winter, American golden plovers lounge in Argentina. As spring begins, the birds head north. They cross the equator in February or March, investigate shorelines and fields in the American heartland through April, then make a grand tour up the center of Canada and cross the Arctic Circle around the first of June. Barely two months later many start traveling south, not retracing their steps, but heading East for a gathering in Labrador, then flying to Brazil and gradually making their way back to Argentina.

Meanwhile, chickadees at your feeders will crisscross the neighborhood thousands of times on a myriad of busy errands. They'll fly here to scold a roosting owl, there for a drink, and back to your feeder for a snack. During migration, they won't travel anywhere, except to accompany warblers, vireos and other small birds migrating through their few acres of homeland. In summer the chickadees will cover their territory in detail hunting for insects to feed the family. And every night of the year the chickadees will go to roost in an old woodpecker hole or a bird box exhausted from their daily efforts, but they will never have gotten out of the neighborhood.

Where will your year take you?

A cedar waxwing reaches for a red fruit—shriveled, but rich with sugar—from a dwindling winter supply.

In winter, waxwings wander in search of food rather than migrate north and south. When they find a good source such as a mountain ash, holly, or hawthorn tree laden with fruit, they'll stay in the area until the produce is gone, and then leave. So you may see dozens of these itinerants one day, and the next day none.

Waxwings process food rapidly. Seeds from fruits and berries may be expelled in as little as 20 minutes after consumption.

The time of day is a statement about the earth's relation to the sun. Two centuries ago local communities based their time on "high noon" —the time when the sun crossed the local meridian, or highest point in the sky. Each community had its own True Local Time. At Noon in Boston, for example, it was only 11:48 a.m. in New York City. Walking or riding a horse from one community to another was such a slow process, widespread down-to-the-minute synchronization was irrelevant. Then trains multiplied travel speed more than 10-fold, and timing became a big issue. At one point, U.S. railways had to keep track of 300 True Local Times. The need for railways to simplify schedules was instrumental in organizing the world's present time zones.

The highly streamlined pintail can cover 400 miles or more in a single migratory flight.

Pintails were once America's most abundant duck after the mallard. They especially thrived in Western states and provinces. In the 1950's they numbered over 10 million, but by the late 1980s their population had dropped by 75 percent. Over time, conservation projects already underway to re-establish western wetlands should increase pintail numbers, hopefully to at least half of the 1950s figures.

As Earth spins on its axis, a point on the equator is traveling more than 1,035 miles per hour. A fighter jet heading west could keep pace with the sun, and theoretically fly all day at high noon. Further north, points on earth move more slowly. At the 45th degree of latitude (think Minneapolis), a commercial jet heading west at about 525 miles per hour could likewise keep pace with the sun. A pintail flying westward with a strong tailwind could keep up with the sun somewhere around the 85th degree of latitude, which is at the top of Greenland.

Above: A displaying ruffed grouse. Opposite: A ruffed grouse walks amidst stems in a forest clearing. The stems will soon grow into the sort of thickets that grouse love.

In the early and mid-20th century, ruffed grouse were one of America's top game birds, with three to four million harvested annually. Their amazing acceleration when flushed and reckless flight speed through thick cover make them perhaps the hardest target of all wild game.

Like a grouse flying though a thicket, sometimes we don't have time to think —we need split-second response. Our subconscious provides the quickest reactions. Consider what happens when someone leaps from behind a doorjamb and says "Boo!" We jump. Then a split second later we realize we've been fooled. The "boo" goes through two paths in our brain for processing. The quickest, subconscious path sends the signal directly to the amygdale, which is a part of the brain that gives feedback to our nerves and produces a response—a reflexive jump and surge of adrenaline. The second path sends the stimulus to the sensory cortex, where it's analyzed more closely, and a second-step response is developed —which in this case identifies the stimulus as a false alarm. The cortex sends this processed signal to the amygdale as well, which then directs us to relax, and wait for that unpleasant surge of adrenaline to dissipate.

Despite its reputation as a harbinger of spring, the robin is probably worse than a groundhog as a seasonal indicator because some robins persist across northern states all winter long.

How much time does a bird have in this world? For songbirds, typically two-thirds of young leaving a nest perish within 12 months. After that first deadly year, the rate of attrition slows roughly by half (so only one out of three birds die in each subsequent year). Still, to become "old" a songbird has to beat stiff odds. For example, if 1,000 robins fledge in your area, statistically only 333 will live a full year, 223 of those will survive a second year, and 149 will manage to fly through their third year. By the end of the seventh year, only 30 of the 1,000 fledglings remain. After year 15, statistics suggest that only one single hardy individual still has time left, and it will die before finishing its 16th year. The oldest robin on record was a captive that reached 17.

A human born before the 20th century faced an average lifespan of less than 45 years. Modern life has miraculously slowed the human clock—at least in first world nations, where human longevity extends nearly eight decades. For birds and other wildlife—and mankind in many parts of the world—the natural clock remains unchanged.

> *Grow old along with me!*
> *The best is yet to be,*
> *The last of life, for which the first*
>   *was made…*
> —Robert Browning

A common redpoll spends winters in bitterly cold, snow-covered fields
and thickets, where it helps define the term "northern bird."

This little goldfinch relative can withstand colder temperatures than any other songbird. It even bathes in snow if open water is not available. Redpolls are so confiding that they have been caught by hand from feeders. In winter, they gather into large flocks.

In 1884 an international conference of 27 nations established time zones. The conference divided the earth longitudinally into 24 units of 15 degrees each. The observatory at Greenwich, England, was declared the starting point, or prime meridian. Each zone east of Greenwich would add one hour; each zone to the west would subtract one hour from Greenwich Mean Time.

This theoretical division has not been perfectly executed. Time Zones tend to wander around the map like a child's drawing because they often follow political borders instead of lines of longitude. In addition, some places simply march to the beat of a different pendulum. While the East Coast of the U.S. is minus five hours from Greenwich, most of the East Coast of Canada is minus four and a half hours. All of India and a central swath of Australia also operate 30 minutes off from a whole hour, and all of China has just one time zone. Even more intriguing is Nepal, which is +5:45 from Greenwich Mean Time.

Over half of the tundra swan's feathers are on its head and long neck, where they ward off cold as the bird dabbles for aquatic vegetation in northern lakes.

The tundra swan leads the feather count for American birds—with over 25,000 feathers. Ruby-throated hummingbirds sit at the other end of the pillow-filling scale with only 1,200 feathers. Most songbirds have 2,000 to 4,000 feathers, which make up less than 10 percent of the birds' weight.

When we look up at the stars at night we're seeing back in time. The nearest star visible to the naked eye, Alpha Centauri, is 4.24 light years away. The twinkling light we see from it left the star more than four years ago. The farthest star in the Milky Way galaxy lies 100,000 light years away. Its light left as homo-sapiens first walked the earth. The nearest galaxy visible to the naked eye, Andromeda, lies 2.2 million light years away. It shows us part of the universe as it was more than 2 million years ago. Some telescopes today can see so far, they look billions of years into the past, virtually to the beginning of our universe. On a clear night, perhaps we really can see forever.

Tired of counting sheep? Think of owls instead, who embrace life under starlight.
But your dreams might not be in color; owls see in black and white.

Owls have few color-sensitive cones in their eyes, which allows them to have a maximum number of light-sensitive rods. Their special eyesight enables them to hunt even on the darkest, moonless nights.

The moon takes 27.3 days to orbit Earth, but we see a full moon only every 29.5 days. Why? While the moon travels around Earth, Earth is traveling around the sun. During the 27.3 days the moon takes for one revolution, Earth travels through 27 degrees of its own orbit. This changes the angle of the sun in relation to the earth and moon, and the moon needs more than two days to "catch up" to the proper angle to again shine full.

The earth has not always spun 29.5 times between full moons. Earth once turned on its axis faster, and a billion years ago, a day was only 19 hours long. In another billion years, Earth's day will stretch to 30 hours. Earth is slowing down because the moon's gravity reaches out to Earth and ever so slightly creates a drag. This drag slows Earth's rotation by about 1/500 of a second per century. Some day in the future Earth's rotation will slow to the point where Earth and her moon synchronize, and gaze at each other with unchanging faces for the rest of time.

Sandhill cranes have been setting their wings for landings for 10 million years.

Water covers 7 of every 10 acres of Earth's surface. Gulls, pelicans, ducks and other waterway and wetland birds take up about a third of a field guide. Perhaps it's not surprising that fish species around the world outnumber all bird species by three to one.

Archaeopteryx *began flying at least 140 million years ago, and eventually shared the world with a number of other avian prototypes. Most of these early birds disappeared with dinosaurs. However, vestiges managed to hold on and provide the genetic base for today's species. Some of North America's most primitive birds—loons and grebes, for instance—can follow their lineage back without much change to the Age of Dinosaurs. The avian world since the fall of dinosaurs has been the scene of tremendous change. Perhaps one-and-a-half million species of birds have come and gone in the past 70 million years. Nearly 10,000 species inhabit the world today*

*Soaring effortlessly on the wind, eagles seem blissfully ignorant of the
myriad of dreams, schemes and sorrows of the people below.*

Despite their place in American culture, bald eagles did not receive official federal legal protection until June, 1940. Ironically, not long thereafter, beginning in the 1950s, bald eagles suffered the most severe threat ever to their existence: widespread use of DDT. Happily, bald eagles have recovered nicely.

In a case of uncanny timing, a massive bald eagle nest in an elm tree along the shores of Lake Erie—one of the last remaining nests in that part of the nation—fell within moments of when President Kennedy was shot. The nest had been in use for more than 30 years and weighed an estimated two tons.

The bald eagle became our national emblem in 1782. That may seem like ancient history, but consider this: Eagles more than 20 years old are common. Following the family tree of just a dozen generations of 20 year old birds would reach back to the days when Ben Franklin was lobbying for wild turkeys to represent this land. A human octogenarian has been alive through a third of the nation's existence.

"Reminiscences make one feel so deliciously aged and sad."
—George Bernard Shaw

The tiny, fidgety golden-crowned kinglet is as busy as the second hand on a watch.

How long is a second? It depends on how it is measured. Originally, a second was determined by true solar time, which is based on Earth's rotation on its axis, and measures the time elapsed between two consecutive noons. A second is 1/86,400 part of that day. Because Earth's axis tilts and its path around the sun is elliptical, solar days vary by nearly half an hour through the year. Scientists corrected the problem by using "mean solar time." However, Earth's axis also wobbles slightly, so even with corrections applied, mean solar time produces a day with an error of up to three milliseconds.

A more accurate measurement is based on Earth's orbit, which is relatively stable. A second defined this way is 1/315,569,259,747th part of that trip. Nevertheless, this measurement also has error. If we had started keeping time a century ago with a clock using corrected mean solar time, and a clock using Earth-orbit, the two timepieces would now be about a minute apart.

In 1972, the official duration of a second became based on the vibrations of cesium atoms in the atomic clock. Atomics clocks have now become so refined that the measurement of a second is, according to the U.S. Naval Observatory, "the most accurate realization of a unit that mankind has yet achieved."

Wear raingear when looking for the varied thrush, which haunts wet northwest coniferous forests.

The varied thrush looks like a party-dressed robin, and sings a unique tune. It voices a single monotone note that sounds like a toy whistle, then 10 seconds later whistles another note, but on a different pitch, then 10 seconds later another, again on a different pitch, and so on. The varied thrush is easier to hear than see because it likes to stay in dense woods.

Have you ever wondered what a particular radio announcer looks like? The appearance of a DJ is often surprising—the DJ does not look at all like we imagined. The avian world is full of audio/visual surprises, too. Consider the bald eagle. Its squeaky, whinny-like chirps seem weak and silly for a bird of such magnificent stature. By contrast, the edgy scream of a red-tailed hawk is a nice fit. Then there are thrushes. Who would suspect the beauty of the hermit thrush song when looking at such a drab brown bird, or for that matter, the strange song of the varied thrush? Some wrens are loud way beyond their size. And how can so many sparrows, which look so similar, make so many different sounds? Beyond that, why do so many birds that don't look like robins sound like them? Wouldn't it be handy if birds resembled their songs?

When food is plentiful, common barn owls nest almost any time of year.
These young are about to make short work of a pocket gopher.

The common barn owl is one of 12 species in the world's barn owl family, and occurs widely around the globe. Among distinctive barn owl features is the heart-shaped—not round—facial disk. This disk not only makes the owl's face resemble a monkey's, it also improves their hearing to such an extent that barn owls can hunt by sound alone.

By chance, we live at a time when the moon and sun appear to be the same size in the sky; they each span roughly five degrees of the heavens and are about the size of a thumbnail on an outstretched arm. However, the moon is moving away from the Earth nearly one-and-one-half inches per year. In time, the moon will no longer cover the sun during an eclipse, and even the brightest moonlit night will remain dark.

The flicker spends as much time hunting food from the ground with its slightly curved bill as from trees.

Nearly half of the flicker's diet consists of ants. Arthur Bent's *Life History of North American Birds* reports that one flicker was collected (shot for scientific study) with 3,000 ants in its stomach, and another with 5,000!

"It [my interest] happened in the 7th grade when I was about 11 years old, and my teacher started a Junior Audubon Society. She gave each of us a box of watercolors and a brush, and a color plate from Fuertes *Birds of New York*. She gave me the blue jay. I thought I did very well, and was distraught when another student got credit for my drawing. Fortunately, that matter was quickly settled. Then the critical moment was the following weekend when a friend and I went to explore new territory south of town. There on the trunk of a tree was a clump of brown feathers. Actually, it was a flicker that was asleep, tired from migration. I thought it was dead, and very gingerly I poked it. It woke up with these wild eyes, and flashed away with those golden wings. It was the contrast between what seemed to be a dead thing, and something that was very much alive that struck me; and ever since then birds have seemed to me to be the most vivid expression of life." —*Roger Tory Peterson, 1992 interview for the* BirdWatch *television show.*

A flock of shorebirds visits exposed flats in a San Francisco Bay estuary while the tide is out.

For some birders, shorebirds are the only kinds of birds to watch. Others prefer raptors. Still others relish the sound and color presented by warblers in the spring. Tastes in birds among birders are as varied as tastes in art. Fortunately, in birds, as in art, there is plenty of variety to go around.

The moon's effect on tides is more than twice as strong as the sun's because the sun is so distant (388 times farther away than the moon). An average high tide in the open ocean creates a water bulge that stands about three feet above low tide. In shallow, narrow bays the bulge gets squeezed and increases in height—up to 50 feet in Canada's Bay of Fundy. On average, high or low tides occur about 50 minutes later each day.

Some days truly drag on, while others fly by. During a year, the noontime sun can arrive as much as 16 minutes early or 14 minutes late. Only four days a years are exactly 24 hours long as measured by the sun. These days occur on or about April 15, June 14, August 31, and December 25.

An indigo bunting sings from atop a spiderwort plant.

In spring, birds present a non-stop stream of songs, chips, calls, scolds, hoots and other noises. Perhaps only politicians and talk-show hosts vocalize more. More than any other season, Spring seems to run on two different clocks...one set by Earth's orbit around the sun, the other by weather. Like the proverbial broken watch that is right twice a day, the weather clock eventually hits right for the season.

Fewer than a dozen specimens of *Archaeopteryx* have been discovered, all between 100 and 150 million years old. *Archaeopteryx* appear to be the first creatures to wear feathers, and provide a bridge between reptiles and birds.

The order *Passeriformes*, or perching birds, has long been considered the newest group in the lineage. However, genetic testing shows so much diversity in the order that it suggests *passerines* date back to the Eocene (50 to 60 million years ago), along with a great many other avian families. *Passeriformes* continue to change today, and currently dominate the bird world on land, accounting for over half of Earth's bird species.

The handsome, talented rose-breasted grosbeak sings a melodic version of a robin's song.
It also has a one syllable call that sounds like the squeak of a sneaker sliding on a gym floor.

People talk to express all sorts of things: happiness; sadness; affection; new ideas. Our thoughts flood out of us in a complex river of communication. Perhaps the same is true for birds. A season of song might cover every topic in their world. Some bird in the yard, unbeknownst to us, might even be a truly creative avian Shakespeare.

On the other hand, avian plagiarists are well-documented. Mockingbirds have been known to mimic more over 30 species in 10 minutes.

In the 1930s the world was surprised by research of Margaret Morse Nice that clearly showed pairs of song sparrows in her neighborhood were not always faithful. Both males and females cheated with shocking regularity. In a more recent study of barn swallows, females readily had "affairs" with any male that had better plumage than her mate. DNA testing now shows that at least 20 percent of the young in any given warbler nest have different fathers.

By the time you say you're his,
Shivering and sighing
And he vows his passion is
Infinite, undying—
Lady, make note of this:
One of you is lying.

—Dorothy Parker

One tree swallow shares thoughts with another.

Birds undoubtedly perceive time on their own scale. Just as high speed movie cameras can take hundreds of frames per second, small birds probably detect several distinct events during the time we see just one. This perhaps helps swallows snag flying insects as a matter of course. And birds such as kinglets and hummingbirds seem to jerk—rather than turn—their heads to look around. (But what looks like a rapid jerk to us might well be a quite leisurely look to the birds!)

Time perception is a personal, intuitive matter, and sometimes bizarrely so. Oliver Sacks, a researcher at a neurological institute often noticed a patient with severe Parkinson's disease with his hand poised somewhere between his side and face. Sacks eventually asked the patient what he was doing, and the patient replied that he was wiping his nose. The surprised researcher, who was an avid amateur photographer, took a series of time-lapse pictures of the patient through the course of one morning, and yes, over a span of several hours the patient's hand eventually went up to and down from his nose. To the patient, the speed of his arm seemed normal.

Audubon called the flashy peregrine falcon the "big-footed falcon."

Diving on flying prey, peregrine falcons curl their feet into fists and clobber, rather than grab, their target. The falcon usually circles back and snatches the falling prey before it hits the ground.

Peregrines are legendary for their diving speed, which can exceed 175 miles per hour. The fastest bird on the straightaway is the white-throated swift, where 100 mph is not unusual in courtships and other displays. Famous for their lack-of-speed are woodcock, which may be our slowest flying bird. During part of their courtship ritual they stay aloft at speeds reported as slow as five mph. House sparrows also are notably slow, fluttering along at about 15 mph. By contrast, a robin cruises at about 25 mph. Most birds can vary flight speed by a factor of at least two. (Rain drops fall at about 14 miles per hour. Olympic sprinters reach speeds of almost 25 miles per hour.)

Vladimir: That passed the time.
Estragon: It would have passed in any case.
Vladimir: Yes, but not so rapidly.
—Samuel Beckett
Waiting for Godot

*Spring migration ends at a nest. Just as instincts guided a bird to and from foreign lands,
they now help build, step-by-step, a brand new nursery.*

In spring, billions of wild birds in North America lay eggs. It's been estimated that at the height of summer, after all eggs hatch, the continent's bird population swells to as many as 20 billion individuals. That's about 60 birds per person. (This may still be less than half of all the birds that once inhabited North America; as one estimate for the number of the extinct passenger pigeon placed it at well over 20 billion birds.)

While our wild birds are busy, so are domestic ones. An average laying chicken hen produces more than 260 eggs a year. Annually, Americans eat 75 billion chicken eggs, or roughly 250 per person per year. We have some of these in the morning before going out to watch birds. Fried, scrambled, boiled, or observed fully feathered and developed months after hatching, bird eggs are an integral part of our world.

The science of time and timekeepers (clocks and watches) is called horology. An antiquarian horologist is an expert on clocks from the past.

A red-winged blackbird sings in dawn's early light.

The dawn chorus, a famous crescendo of bird song, starts at first light on spring mornings. Species join the songfest in a predictable order. Birds with the largest eyes sing first, and those with eyes that gather less light follow as the world grows brighter. The noisy, busy chorus usually fades in less than half an hour.

A study of male black-capped chickadees also shows that, at least for them, the early morning birds may not get the worm, but enjoy other rewards. Newly awakened males usually sing near a roosting female, encouraging her to awake, and join him for mating.

Time marches to the beat of two different drums. The first drum has rhythmic and cyclic cadences: the beat of waves washing ashore; sunrise and sunset; the cycle of the moon; the changing seasons. The second drum has unpredictable hits with no rhythm. Beats come on the occasion of one-time events: the sighting of a new bird for the list; a graduation; a birth; a death. These are the accents and cymbal strikes of life. With luck, they have a pleasing sound.

Fishing is one of America's favorite pastimes. Plenty of birds fish, too—herons, egrets, mergansers, kingfishers, pelicans, and owls are all terrific anglers.

Owls fishing? Yes. The barred owl, for example, in southern swamps fishes routinely, but it's more apt to catch the bait—crayfish—than fish. This author once saw a great horned owl deliver a hand-sized crappie to her nestlings. The front half of the fish had already been eaten—which meant the streamlined part of the fish was gone. One of the nestlings, in typical owl fashion, set upon swallowing the fish whole in one grand snake-like swallow. The young bird fought that blunt-fronted fish for at least half an hour before finally landing it in its crop.

Snowy owls sometimes feed char (a trout-like fish of the far north) to their young, especially when lemming populations are low.

Screech owls are also noted anglers. The bird in the photograph regularly served minnows to a nest of young. On warm evenings the adults delivered moths, beetles, and other insects to the nestlings, but on cold nights insects were hard to find and the owls went fishing. The adults carried the fish in their beaks, but usually their feet and leg feathers were still wet and dripping when they got to the nest.

An eastern bluebird wonders what happened to all the insects it put into mouths just seconds ago.

*M*e casa es su casa. Welcome to my home. In our world of cities and suburbs many birds still find plenty of hospitality… a comfortable perch here, a nice tuft of nest grass there, and birds are a rare breed of guest. Even if they make themselves right at home, we still hope they never leave.

While Daylight Saving Time is supposed to save energy by balancing use of electric lights with daylight, it can also create confusion. Usually, a state government decides what time zone to use and whether or not to observe daylight saving time. But in Indiana, until recently, each county got to choose its time zone. Most opted for the Eastern Time Zone, but a handful of western ones jumped to the Central Time Zone in order to stay in step with Chicago. In addition, the majority of Eastern Time counties did NOT observe daylight saving time, but some did. So, Indiana had two time zones with localized observation of daylight saving. This caused various regions across the state to blink in and out of synchronization in a confusing three-way follow-the-clock shell game. Recent state actions have helped simplify the system.

A Carolina chickadee tends to its family.

From New Jersey to Kansas, chickadees seem to observe an invisible fence. To the north live black-capped chickadees, and to the south are Carolina chickadees. The two species look a lot alike, act a lot alike, share the same type of habitat and sometimes even breed together. But they don't invade each other's breeding range. What mechanism—besides the fact chickadees are essentially non-migratory—protects the purity of their species, even though they rub shoulders across an interface that's a thousand miles long and lacks an apparent geographic barrier?

It seems that hybrids are the unwitting border guards because they suffer low fertility. Female hybrids rarely produce young. Nests produced by hybrid males produce far fewer young than those with pedigreed parents, and the resultant genetic line gets swamped. Interestingly, the width of the band where hybrid chickadees form part of the breeding population is generally narrow – less than a dozen miles wide in the part of Ohio where one study took place. This study also showed that while some genes do indeed get across this border and can be found a hundred miles or more from the line, the seepage is not enough to upset the integrity of either species. The authors describe the border between the species as not exactly a wall, but more like a transparent semipermeable membrane.

Based on "Reproductive Success Across the Hybrid Zone in Ohio", by C. L. Bronson et al; THE AUK. Vol 122, No. 3.

Yahoo! At some point in our life, there is always a leap into the unknown. One-day-old wood ducks get it over early.

If wood duck babies could see all the predator mouths that will be open wide during the next few weeks, they might not leap. However, for the lucky ducky that survives until autumn, the future looks bright. Waterfowl have notably long lives that span decades—if they can just get past that first summer hurdle.

How long can any life last? In the world of plants the answer is a long, long time. A bristlecone pine in the White Mountains of California is almost 5,000 years old. Much of the trunk of this gnarled veteran is dead, but a few green branches and healthy roots carry on the spark of life. Part of the secret of its longevity is that the trees live at the edge of the tree-line, in a cold, dry climate where they lie dormant nine months of the year.

Some creosote bushes in California tally in at 12,000 years old. The bushes form a circle around their genetic source, a single plant, which before disappearing sent out runners. These runners sent out other runners, and so on, and the creosote bush has been perpetually alive since the last ice age.

Vertebrates get considerably fewer grains of sand for their timer. The oldest known living vertebrate is a 175 year old turtle on the Galapagos. Some parrots can live a century. The record-holder dog made it 29 years.

Suited in torrid colors, the painted bunting spends summers in steamy southeastern and south-central states.

Birds seem to wear every style and color of garment in the closet. Some wear bright solids, others more somber hues. Bold patches of color are popular, yet so are soft intricate patterns. Still others wear gaudy accents like fashion jewelry. As with trends of fashion, bird attire sometimes is hard to explain.

Birds such as killdeer that have exposed nests in hot climates must sometimes cool the eggs rather than warm them. The adults may simply make shade or, by moistening breast feathers, provide additional cooling through evaporation.

Birds don't sweat. They loose heat by panting. Moist air in the lungs and throat gathers heat, and both heat and air are expelled together. In general, birds die more quickly from exposure to heat than to cold.

"By the time I was six, having concluded that there were no tigers or comets or dinosaurs in our hum-drum Indiana neighborhood, I had turned to birds as the best thing available."
—Kenn Kaufman
Kingbird Highway

Mrs. and Mr. (left to right) Acorn Woodpecker take a moment to
"get away from it all" and have a drink—at a sugar water feeder in Arizona.

Few birds leave legacies for future generations, but acorn woodpeckers create a granary—a tree for storing acorns. The tree is excavated with thousands of small, shallow holes just the right size for holding acorns from the local species of oak. In the fall, a family clan of woodpeckers stocks this larder, then aggressively defends it. The granary is used for as long as it stands, a time that may span several woodpecker generations.

Time lapse and slow motion photography give us a remarkable ability to visually expand and compress time almost at will. For example, in time lapse the many minutes a gull takes to swallow a starfish could be watched in seconds. In 1895, only a few years after Edison presented the world's first movies, H.G. Wells wrote his remarkable Time Machine, *where the Time Traveler vividly describes the world in time lapse: "I saw the sun hopping swiftly across the sky, leaping it every minute, and every minute marking a day… The slowest snail that ever crawled dashed by too fast for me… Presently, as I went on, still gaining velocity, the palpitation of day and night merged into one continuous grayness… the jerking sun became a streak of fire… The whole surface of earth seemed changed—melting and flowing under my eyes."*

The summer tanager winters in Central and South America, but spends its summers in the southern forests of the U.S.

Ah! The summer sun! At the 45th degree of latitude on the first day of summer there are almost seven more hours of daylight than in winter.

Not only are daylight hours longer in summer, the sunlight is more intense. In fact, the summer sun may have twice as much strength as the winter sun. To see why, shine the beam of a flashlight on a basketball, holding the beam at "equator" level. Note the size of the beam when it falls on the equator. Now, angle the light up towards the pole. The beam spreads over a much larger area, diluting its intensity. In summer, the high over-head sun beams down on us more directly with concentrated power; in winter, the sun stays low in the sky, and its weak angled rays give little warmth. From winter solstice to summer solstice, the sun climbs 47 degrees higher in the sky.

Even in the hottest of places, sunlight does not directly heat air. Instead it heats land, water and other materials (including our skin), which then radiate the energy back out, but at a lower wavelength. This radiated energy does indeed heat the atmosphere—and we look for shade.

Golden eagles leisurely ride wind thermals for hours at a time, but can dive at speeds measured at over 150 miles per hour. Top speed for a typical free-falling human skydiver in the standard prone position with arms and legs bent is about 130 mph, according to the Physics Fact Book, *edited by Glen Elert. By "standing" or "diving," skydivers have reportedly achieved speeds of over 300 miles per hour.*

Golden eagles have an unusually long incubation period of 42 to 45 days. This is a full week longer than that of bald eagles. The albatross leads the world in incubation, with a period of nearly 65 days. A number of songbirds, including vireos, orioles and warblers have incubation periods as short as 11 days.

While birds sit quietly on the nest, seconds steadily tick by on the atomic clock. Most atomic clocks count vibrations of cesium 133 atoms. 9,192,631,770 vibrations make one second. To ensure counting accuracy, over 200 atomic clocks are scattered around the world and their tallies are averaged to make each second the official length.

Cesium atoms march at their own special pace, without regard to Earth's practical time tables based on its rotation around its axis and revolution around the sun. To keep the atomic clock in tune with our seasons, the International Bureau of Weights and Measures every few years adds or subtracts a second from the atomic clock.

Yellow warblers nest across almost the entire continent, where they display unusual powers of perception.

Some of the birds can be fooled some of the time.... A lot of birds don't recognize their own eggs. Cowbirds exploit this oversight by laying their eggs willy-nilly in the nests of other species. Usually the cowbird removes an egg when she lays one. In some cases, the cowbird eggs, which are light brown and spotted on the large end with dark brown, look somewhat similar to the eggs of the unwitting hosts, but other times the appearance is not even close. For example, wood thrush eggs are as blue as robin's, yet wood thrushes routinely hatch cowbird young. One wood thrush was observed incubating a nest with just a single blue egg surrounded by a bouquet of five spotted cowbird eggs.

A few species are harder than others to fool. The yellow warbler is famously persnickety at its nest. If a cowbird lays an egg, the warbler may desert, or sometimes build a new nest on top of the old one. Yellow warbler nests three layers high have been reported.

Domestic birds can be fooled too. A farmer who wants to encourage a chicken to start a clutch might build a nest and put an egg, a golf ball, or even a doorknob in it. For a hen that is even remotely in the mood, it induces a hormonal reaction that results in eggs in a matter of days.

How do baby birds like these ruby-throated hummingbirds decide when its time to leave the nest?

Precocial birds like ducks are ready to leave the nest once they dry out, which is within hours of hatching. However, early hatchers may have to stay put for up to a day, living off residual egg yolk in their body, until all siblings are ready and the mother leads them away.

For many altricial birds, the nest gets disturbingly crowded when young start flexing and flapping wings. One of the nestlings may get pushed out, or leave just to get out of the way. Once away from the nest, a youngster—now a fledgling—almost never goes back. In fact, adults generally lead fledglings away by calling or luring them with food. This spurs other young to follow suit, and within a few hours the nest is vacant. Invariably, all young songbirds in a nest leave on the same day.

For many species, whenever they leave, to our eyes it may seem too soon. Who hasn't tried to stuff a down-tufted, fluttering robin back into the nest, only to be dismayed by the bird's refusal to stay?

A Long-tailed Jaeger at its nest sees the sunny side of tundra life.

In the tropics—that broad swath of earth between the Tropics of Capricorn and Cancer—the length of daylight remains nearly unchanged year round. Nesting seasons for birds are indistinct or determined by the local rainy season.

Heading away from the tropics, the rate of change in the length of daylight grows increasingly large. At the Arctic Circle, the change averages eight minutes per day, but varies widely by season. Right after the winter solstice, daylight grows barely a minute a day but gradually increases, and just before the summer solstice, the sun stays up more than 20 minutes longer every day, until that magical day around June 21st when it never sets.

In a year, every part of earth receives the same amount of daylight. The arctic gets nearly all its quota during spring and summer. Under its extraordinarily long daylight hours, the tundra gets supercharged, and vibrates with life as throngs of migrant birds almost frantically "make hay while the sun shines." Animals living in these rigorous areas even tend to have faster heartbeats than counterparts in the languid tropics.

Trying to identify sparrows can be challenging. The markings of this song sparrow make it blend into the crowd on the pages of a field guide.

The American Ornithologist's Union (AOU) is the official scientific record keeper for North America's birds. The AOU divides the avian clan into species, and assigns names. The AOU Check-List of North American Birds is revised from time to time because species get lumped together or split apart according to new research. Nowadays, DNA evidence seems to weigh the heaviest on the split/not split scale.

There are more than 30 species known by the common name "sparrow" and they can be difficult to differentiate. One of the best ways to identify them is by learning the distinctive song of each species.

Naming seems to be a particularly fickle science. For example, in recent decades a tall white wading bird has been known as the American egret, great egret and common egret, all without the change of a single feather on the bird's part. Its current name is great egret.

For ruby-throated hummingbirds, it's life in the fast lane.

A resting ruby-throated's heart beats ten times a second, or 600 times in a minute. During activity, the heart rate may climb to 1,200 beats per minute. An average wing beat takes about 1/60th of a second (60 cycles per second—or hertz—produces the low hum we hear). The lower limit to human hearing is about 20 hertz. Sixty cycles per second yields 3,600 cycles per minute.

A hummingbird seems to be a real gas guzzler. An average ruby-throat consumes over 15 calories per day. Flower nectar averages about 30 calories per ounce; thus, in the course of a day, a hummingbird consumes over half an ounce of nectar, which is more than five times the bird's weight. The sugar alone equals a full teaspoon of white sugar, which it burns 50 times faster than man. The hummer also eats small insects for protein.

Some ruby-throats fly 600 miles nonstop to cross the Gulf of Mexico in a flight that averages 12 hours. Before setting out, the little birds increase their weight by as much as 50 percent over the typical summer level. A successful 600 mile flight uses barely 2 grams (1/14th of an ounce) of fuel. Hardly a gas guzzler, after all.

This was a noteworthy nest.

Years back, I encountered a nest shared simultaneously by a pair of robins and a pair of cardinals. The nest, created without federal court decisions or other human intervention, involved more than mingling of races. Robins are thrushes and cardinals are finches—they're from different avian families.

The nest held four young robins, and three young cardinals. The living quarters were indeed crowded, and, sad to say, the arrangements may not have been 100 percent harmonious. The nestlings showed no animosity towards one another, but the adults tended to feed only their own.

I can only speculate how the nest developed. The bottom of the nest looked like it was made of loosely assembled sticks, as if a cardinal put it together. The top had a more refined robin-like finish. Robins typically build on a sturdy platform, such as a tree crotch. Cardinals may build days in advance of laying eggs. Perhaps the robins found the cardinal nest was the best available platform (this was in a rather treeless suburb), and moved in while the cardinals paused after construction. By the time all was said and done, neither bird was ready to give up its investment, and both stayed.

I am happy to report that all seven of the young fledged, but I've never again encountered robins and cardinals so thoroughly integrated.

Loons step us back in time.

If one million years equals one human step, 65 or 70 steps takes you back to the time when the first birds that we might recognize today appeared (birds such as loons, grebes, and herons). Another 60 or 70 steps beyond that marks the heyday of *Archaeopteryx*. You would have now walked nearly 1½ football fields.

Walk another four football fields to reach the conclusion of the Cambrian era, which saw a massive explosion of life. As you walk hundreds of yards back through time in the Cambrian era you will encounter the first land animals, the first land plants, fish-like sea creatures in the oceans, and finally, trilobites and numerous other life forms that have ceased to exist today. Before that, traveling even father back into time, you'll encounter mostly blue-green algae in the ocean. The algae released the first free oxygen molecules into the atmosphere.

To go back to a time beyond these first primitive plants you will have to hike a total of about ¾ of a mile. Then for another mile there are primitive globs of living molecules and microbes. Many scientists think the first life appeared on earth roughly 1¾ miles from the first humans if you were to hike back through history, a million-year-step at a time.

Henry Ward Beecher, a 19th century preacher and naturalist, raised the issue of bird intelligence when he claimed that if men wore wings and feathers, very few would be clever enough to be crows.

Few ornithologists would debate that a crow is a smart bird, but its larger cousin, the raven, might be smarter still. Some experts believe that large gulls have even more brainpower. What about North America's stupidest birds? Nobody wants to name names. However, Albert Einstein observed that the difference between genius and stupidity is that genius has limits.

In Einstein's famous equation, E=mc2, c is the speed of light, which is approximately 300,000 kilometers per second. C-squared thus equals (approximately) 90,000,000,000. E (energy) is measured in joules. One joule of energy is enough to lift a small apple up against earth's gravity about one meter. M is measured in kilograms (2.2 lbs.), so this equation shows that a single kilogram of matter converted to energy could lift a basket of 90 billion apples—five times more apples than Americans eat in a year.

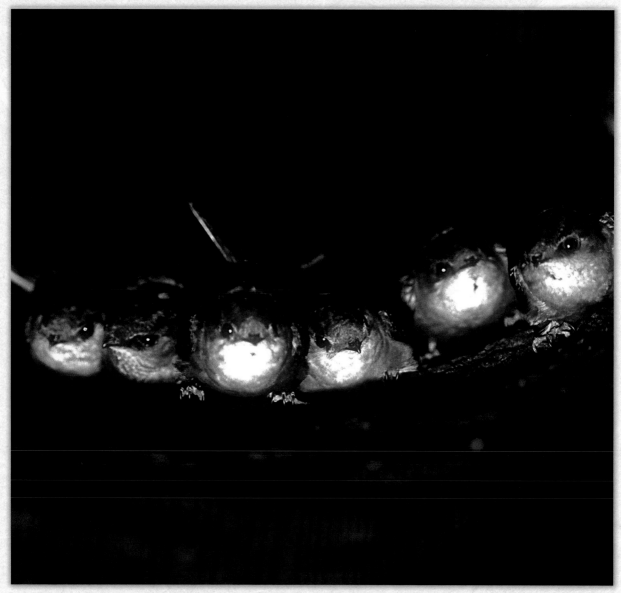

During nesting season, an adult chimney swift may fly more than 500 miles a day. One banded chimney swift is estimated to have flown over a million miles in his nine-year lifespan, including annual round trips to South America.

The crew circumnavigating the globe with Ferdinand Magellan in the early 1500's kept meticulous track of the days of the voyage in journals. They were surprised to learn upon returning home that they were a day behind in their records. They had seen one less sunrise and sunset than had those who had stayed put on land. Later, the concept of time zones would help illustrate what had happened—since they sailed west, they should have detracted an hour from their day for each of the 24 time zones they crossed.

Some terms Magellan would not have known: 1 decisecond=one tenth of a second (truly, a blink-of-the-eye); 1 centisecond=one hundredth of a second (a good stopwatch measures in hundredths of a second); 1 millisecond=one thousandth of a second (a camera shutter speed of a thousandth of a second will capture most human motion); 1 microsecond=one millionth of a second; 1 nanosecond=one billionth of a second (the atomic clock counts more than 9 billion nanoseconds to measure a second; your computer typically uses 3 or 4 nanoseconds to execute one software instruction); 1 picosecond=1 trillionth of a second (this is the shortest time span we can measure with some accuracy).

A diving horned grebe can hold its breath for three minutes.

Throughout Earth's history the oxygen concentration in the atmosphere has varied greatly. In fact, only after plants began releasing it through photosynthesis has oxygen been able to stay in the air at all. Without plants renewing it, atmospheric oxygen is depleted through chemical reactions. For example, earthquakes and erosion expose rocks with minerals like iron that lock it up through oxidation.

Presently, oxygen makes up 21 percent of what we and the birds breathe. During the Carboniferous Period, which ended about 250 million years ago, oxygen climbed steeply from 16 percent to nearly 35 percent (an all-time high). The Period's 60 million year span was characterized by especially large and prolific woody plants that eventually became much of the coal we burn today. The period was also marked by insects super-sized and supercharged from the high volume of oxygen available to them. Some dragonflies were as large as hawks.

Then, in just 10 million years, oxygen concentration was cut in half. The reduction was catastrophic to life, and helped cause wholesale extinctions. What spurred the change is uncertain, but the geologic tumult of mountain building may have played a part.

When oxygen has abounded, life has flourished. Thus, the first birds and dinosaurs appeared during high oxygen periods, then disappeared during drop-offs. For the past 50 million years atmospheric oxygen has been increasing. Who knows how long our canaries will sing?

The great blue heron weighs between five and eight pounds and has a wingspan of up to six feet.

The following are the average weights of some familiar species of birds. And remember, 1 ounce=28 grams; 1 lb.=16 ounces or 454 grams.

Ruby-throated hummingbird: 4g
Magnificent hummingbird: 7.25g
Black-capped chickadee: 11g
Western & Eastern bluebirds: 30g
American robin: 75g
Northern bobwhite: 170g
American crow: 1.2 lbs.
Red-tailed hawk: 2.5 lbs.
Herring gull: 2.5 lbs.
Great blue heron: 5.3 lbs.
Brown pelican: 8.2 lbs.
Bald eagle: 9.4 lbs.
Trumpeter swan: 23 lbs.
Wild turkey: 16.5 lbs. (males—largest gobblers reach up to 30 lbs); hens 9.4 lbs.
Whooping crane: 15 lbs.
California condor: 23 lbs.
A fully loaded Boeing 747 weighs about 850,000 pounds (359 million grams) at take-off.
Birds like the albatross that spend most of their life gliding may have a skeleton that weighs less than their feathers.

This photo of a sanderling shows lots of feather detail. Sometimes we drop a few details for a better perspective.

Pixel is a contraction of "picture element." We use pixels to describe the quality or resolution of a digital picture. If the digital picture gets printed, the pixels become dots. The more pixels—or dots—per inch, the finer the resolution—that is, the greater the detail we can see. For example, in a 300 dots per inch (dpi) photo you might be able to discern individual feathers on a bird, but with 100 dpi the feathers might blur into an undifferentiated matte of color.

Without even thinking about it, we also use a broad range of resolutions for time. For example, a second yields a very high resolution. If we want to gloss over details for a broader look, we jump to minutes, or hours or days. Many people are even familiar with abbreviations such as "BYA" (billions of years ago). Our grasp of time gives us an innate sense of what unit of measurement keeps our computations flowing while giving us a sharp-enough picture.

"Half our life is spent trying to find something to do with the time we have rushed through life trying to save."
—Will Rogers

A blue headed vireo pauses to feed and rest during the day before resuming migration.

Even though most birds usually sleep at night, during migration many wait until well after sundown before flying. Why? According to Michael R. Miller and associates, "Nocturnal atmospheric conditions provide distinct advantages to migrating birds, including cooler temperatures and more humidity, denser air, weaker and more laminar horizontal winds, and little or no vertical air motion compared with daytime conditions; these conditions maximize flight speed while reducing energy cost. Additionally, night migration would enable celestial navigation." (Miller, et al, "Flight Speeds of Northern Pintail" *The Wilson Bulletin* Vol. 117, No.4)

While migratory birds seem to have an innate sense of navigation, people need tools and devices. In 1714 the British government offered a prize to anyone who could develop a means for determining longitude to within half a degree after a voyage from England to the West Indies. In 1761, John Harrison, a carpenter and self-taught clock-maker, finally earned the prize with a spring and balance wheel escapement chronometer that kept time to within about a fifth of a second a day.

The scarlet tanager (above) and the baltimore oriole (opposite) are two of the most brightly colored and most beloved neotropical migrant songbirds that make the trek between North and South America each year.

Two theories try to explain the origin of North America to South America bird migration. One theory says that the ice ages pushed birds far to the south, and when the glaciers retreated, the birds flew north to reclaim their ancestral nesting homes. The second theory says birds from South America flew north to take advantage of the food, shelter, and opportunity offered by our continent in summer.

In the first theory, birds are inherently North American, and only visit South America. In the second theory, our migrant birds are inherently South American. After visiting here for a few months to nest, they fly south to return home.

Life…
whether or not we use it, it goes…
—Phillip Larkin
The Whitsun Weddings

Robins are designed by nature to thrive in yards mowed by Toro.

A German entomologist in Joseph Conrad's book *Lord Jim* says of a butterfly: "Look! The beauty—but that is nothing—look at the accuracy, the harmony. And so fragile! And so strong! And so exact! This is Nature—the balance of colossal forces. Every star is so—and every blade of grass stands so—and the mighty Kosmos in perfect equilibrium produces—this. This wonder, this masterpiece of Nature—the great artist."

Those same colossal forces in Nature, the great artist, have also shaped the robin, but some of us perhaps have a less romantic imagination than Conrad's entomologist, because where he saw the wonder of creation, we see comforting uniformity.

We expect a robin to look like a robin, no matter where we see it, whether in Florida or Alaska. The song it sings should be essentially unchanged, and so, too, should be the manner in which it feeds, nests and flies.

*The American Golden-Plover shares its breeding grounds with the Pacific Golden-Plover
in far western North American tundra regions. It flies up to 20,000 miles per year,
usually including a nonstop flight of 3,000-3,500 miles over the Atlantic.*

Many species nesting in central regions of northern Canada start autumn migration by flying east until they reach the Atlantic, then head south. Every year, however, a few individuals of these species show up along the Pacific Coast instead of the Atlantic. Perhaps these birds are natural "lefties" or just confused east and west. Fortunately, once at the Pacific, the birds invariably head south according to plans.

Some shorebirds, a few warblers, and other migrants that gather in fall in Nova Scotia take a direct, over-water, non-stop 3,000 mile flight to the coast of South America. If they were to leave, say, Friday night after the local high school football game ends, they'll still be flying nonstop on Monday morning when you go to work, and even Monday night when you go to bed. With luck, if they've survived the trip, they'll land, exhausted, as you have a cup of coffee on Tuesday morning.

During the trip birds often climb to nearly 10,000 feet, a height at which humans face a potential for altitude sickness, and commercial jets become pressured. Sometimes birds may reach altitudes of 20,000 feet.

Only about 20 percent of birds nesting in North America are full-time local residents that show no migratory behavior at all. Many species, such as jays, migrate only a few hundred miles.

Travel to new lands can be exciting—and dangerous. As much as 85 percent of mortality for black-throated blue warblers occurs during migration.

Aided by some very tall broadcast towers, the average American spends over three hours a day watching television. It's claimed this sedentary pastime is detrimental to our mental and physical health. Be that as it may, the towers are unquestionably deadly to birds. An estimated five million birds die annually in collisions with communication towers and guy wires. The heaviest mortality occurs during September migration, when small birds fly at night and strike unseen structures and wires. Foggy nights are especially deadly. Over 2,000 birds have been killed at one tower in a single night.

Buildings can be a problem, too. The Washington Monument is one of the lowest structures that has regular impacts from nocturnal migrants. The Empire State building also causes a lot of mortality, so they now douse the lights on peak migration nights in the fall.

On the brighter side of urban life, some birds have learned to take advantage of artificial lighting to extend their "daylight" hours for foraging. For example, a number of diurnal species have been observed "catching flies" around stadium lights at baseball games or searching for food around bushes in well-lit parking lots.

Breathe deeply!

While at rest, most mammals take one breath for every four and a half beats of their heart. Birds breathe less often. Small birds at rest take a breath only every six beats; large birds might breathe once every ten heartbeats.

Birds draw fewer breaths because of the design of their respiratory system. They dedicate four times more body volume to air exchange than mammals and they handle air flow more efficiently.

Mammals breathe with tidal flows of air—air comes and goes in the same place. This leaves residue of low-oxygen air lingering in the lungs. Birds, on the other hand, put only fresh air into their lungs. Newly captured air first goes directly into special air sacs where it's held until the next breath. Then it flows into the lungs where the oxygen is claimed; afterwards, this stale air is sent into another set of air sacs, where it awaits final discharge on the fourth breath. Because this one-way system saturates lungs with only fresh air, it allows the lungs to be smaller—and lighter.

Efficient lungs help give birds the extra oomph they need to flap their wings and fly high—without even breathing hard.

While our autumn harvest proceeds against brilliant backdrops of fall foliage,
thrushes quietly lurk in shadows picking fruits and berries.

Often the first produce to be harvested by birds in fall has high fat content, like these bright red spicebush berries. The fat makes the berries prone to spoilage, but countless thrushes and other frugiverous migrants hungry for energy ensure few go to waste.

Migrating birds share the air with a myriad of electromagnetic waves from radio and TV broadcasters. These invisible waves travel in up-and-down sine waves, sort of like the up-and-down flight of goldfinches flying across a field. If we could see these waves, their size might surprise us. An FM station broadcasting at 90.1 on the dial has a wavelength measuring 10 feet.

When America's astronauts launch, all chronometers are set to use mission elapsed time. However, the International Space Station uses Greenwich Mean Time (GMT). If our astronauts dock to or enter the space station they convert to GMT. Then, upon leaving the station, they switch back to mission elapsed time

The graceful white-crowned sparrow flies fast, relatively speaking.

The shaft of flight feathers is always cheated towards the feather's leading edge. This causes a natural, flight-enhancing rotation of feathers as a bird flies. On upstrokes, feathers rotate "open" so air passes through them easily. On down strokes, feathers rotate in the opposite direction to present maximum surface pushing against the air. Tail feathers and most other feathers not directly involved in flight propulsion have shafts down the middle.

Time—about 100 years of it—has not made Einstein's special theory of relativity any easier to understand. Fortunately most of us can watch birds and live productive lives without fully understanding it. Reassurance is provided by Stanford's Linear Accelerator, a high tech lab devoted to particle physics and understanding how time, space, matter, energy, and speed relate to one another. An official statement from the lab explains, "The laws [describing the behavior of moving objects] are different at speeds reached by particles in Accelerators... For particles moving at slow speeds (very much less than the speed of light) Newton's laws provide a very good approximate form... the differences between Einstein's laws of motion and those derived by Newton are tiny... Einstein's theory supersedes Newton's, but Newton's theory provides a very good approximation for objects moving at everyday speeds."

Blue jays and squirrels have different approaches to acorn storage.

Blue jays pick a certain area of a woods for stashing acorns and other seeds. They probably don't recall exactly where each acorn is hidden, but they remember the area of the stash. To find acorns in winter, they'll hunt there. Squirrels, on the other hand, take a more random approach. They bury acorns everywhere, and later find them by smell. Jays, woodpeckers, squirrels, turkeys, deer, bears and other animals, including insects, eat at least 95 percent of the annual acorn crop.

Earth's revolution around the sun takes 365.2425 days. Because of those extra digits tagged on at the end of 365 (which amount to roughly a half-dozen hours), without correction, in just over 750 years our calendar would be 180 degrees out of touch with the seasons. It would snow in St. Louis on July 4th. The Gregorian calendar we use provides correction by adding leap days every four years, except in years divisible by 100, unless that year is also divisible by 400. (1800 and 1900 were not leap years, but 2000 was). Because of this 400 rule, the calendar precisely repeats only every 400 years. During those four centuries, the 13th of the month falls on Friday 688 times, more times than any other day of the week.

Tufted titmice collect animal hair for lining nests… and sometimes provide a thread for binding souls.

The following is told by Keith "Catfish" Sutton, a leading authority on catching catfish.

"My father and mother divorced when I was five years old, and soon after, my mom, sister and I moved from our home in Delaware to live with my maternal grandmother in Arkansas. I didn't see my father again for almost ten years. As a consequence, I don't remember many things about my father that took place during my early childhood.

"One glimmering from the past stands out, however. I can clearly remember sitting at a window with my dad and watching tufted titmice coming and going from a feeder he and I had built. That was almost half a century ago, so my memory might be failing me when it suggests we sometimes sat for hours watching those little gray birds gleaning seeds. More likely, the times we spent birdwatching lasted only a few minutes each. I am absolutely certain, however, those moments I spent sitting in my father's lap in front of the feeder were the beginning of a lifelong love of birds and birdwatching.

"We never knew each other well, my father and I. But in his later years, while fishing one day, I told him about my memories of the feeder and the titmice. A tear came to his eye as he listened. That was the only time I ever saw him cry."

A canvasback gets ready to land on the Chesapeake Bay, an area long famous for waterfowl and waterfowl hunting.

In *The Floating Opera*, a novel about life in a small town on Chesapeake Bay, John Bath puts forth the idea that we learn about our friends as if they were performing a drama on a boat floating in a tidal river. As we sit on shore the boat comes and goes from view with the ebb and flow of the tide. From the parts of the drama we see in front of us, we think we know what is going on in our friends' lives, but by no means do we know the entire story.

Similarly, birds enter and leave our view on a schedule of their own. Often we strain to see more of them with the suspicion that surprising things may happen out of sight.

To help we buy binoculars and telescopes; we travel, talk, read and photograph; we devote time, energy and resources.

The world of birds and people is full of surprises. Who knows who will next get married, or divorced, or go to jail; or show up way out of place on a journey nobody understands.

"It seems that I have spent my entire time trying to make life more rational and that it was all wasted effort."
—A.J. Ayer

Birds are not always as happy as larks.

North American avian history has had some disturbing times, including:

Mid 1800s: Great Auks go extinct. These flightless, penguin-like birds lived along the Atlantic coast and along parts of Europe. Sailors devastated colonies for meat and eggs, and introduced predators such as rats.

1851-1852: One hundred house sparrows are introduced into Brooklyn.

Late 1870s: Labrador Ducks go extinct. In all fairness, humans may have only been a helper in the process of extinction of this uncommon duck of the northeast, about which little is known.

Early 1890s: About 100 European starlings are released into New York's Central Park by people who want to introduce into America all the bird species Shakespeare mentions. Though earlier attempts to establish starlings failed, this one did not.

1917: Martha, the last known passenger pigeon, dies in the Cincinnati Zoo. Passenger pigeons in North America probably once numbered in the billions.

1918: Incas, a Carolina Parakeet also in captivity in the Cincinnati Zoo, dies. A small flock of wild birds is reported in the 1920s, but the species is never again seen. They formerly nested across the south Atlantic and gulf states, and migrated as far north as Wisconsin.

1932: A heath hen, a prairie chicken relative on the East Coast, is sighted for the last time.

Early 1960s: Bachman's warblers of the Southeast disappear, probably forever.

A Cooper's hawk eats a pigeon in a suburban yard.

Cooper's and Sharp-shinned hawks show an interesting division of zip codes in and around Terre Haute, Indiana. The two closely-related predators look and act much alike, but the Cooper's is larger.

The division became apparent when ornithologists tried to compare natural versus man-related mortality for the hawks in urban and rural areas. The researchers found very few Sharp-shinneds in urban habitat, despite the abundance of appropriate sized prey, such as sparrows. Conversely they found few Cooper's in rural areas.

The researchers surmised that great horned owls made the difference. The owls lived only in rural habitat. Apparently their inclination to kill hawks made rural habitat distinctly less desirable. Naturally, the prime owl-free urban real estate was claimed by the dominant birds—the Cooper's hawks.

(Based on "Survival of Wintering Accipiters," Roth et al; *The Wilson Bulletin*, Vol. 117, No. 3.)

"Life is a great surprise. I do not see why death should not be an even greater one."

—Vladimir Nabakov

Shooting a flying duck is a matter of instinct and timing—and luck.

The shotgun pellets of a typical duck hunter have a muzzle velocity of about 1,400 feet per second. To cover 40 yards—a nice range—the shot takes almost 0.1 second (this includes drop in speed from wind resistance). After 40 yards, 70 percent of the pellets remain within a 30-inch circle.

Meanwhile, a duck's flight speed can vary from 15 mph to over 50 mph. At 15 mph, while the pellets travel, the duck will cover about two feet; at 50 mph, the duck will travel over seven feet.

To hit a moving target, the hunter has to "swing" with it to pick up its path. Then he has to lead the target so the shot will intercept it. If the bird's speed or distance is miscalculated, the 30-inch pattern provides little margin for error. A fast duck may fly three times the width of the pattern while pellets travel from the gun.

All this is vastly more complicated by the fact that from the hunter's perspective, the speed of the duck appears to change as it approaches, flies by, and departs. While the duck approaches, the hunter swings the gun slowly, because the bird is not making much lateral progress. As the duck moves into range, its speed seems to increase dramatically because the bird's movement is now taking it past, instead of towards the hunter. Then, after the duck goes by it seems to slow down again, leaving the hunter wondering why he missed such an easy shot.

The same speed deception occurs for photographers with a camera, who will find it surprisingly hard to get a good shot of a flying bird.

Crossbills have bizarre mandibles that cross at the end, providing a perfect tool for prying open evergreen cones. They slip their tongue into the opened cone to extract the seed.

North America has two species of crossbills—white-winged and red. Some ornithologists believe red crossbills could and should be split into more than half a dozen species, because various groups of these birds differ in size, feeding habits, calls and range. However, one factor that probably will not play a role in a future splitting of the species is whether the bill crosses to the right or to the left. Left-crossed and right-crossed red crossbills occur in about equal numbers and there seems to be little genetic linkage to the crossing side.

Our seasons are not of equal duration. In the Northern Hemisphere, spring runs 93 days, summer 94 days, fall 90 days and winter a relatively brief 89 days. The differences develop from the fact that Earth's orbit is slightly elliptical, and the sun is a little off-center towards one end of the ellipse. As Earth travels through her orbit, and as the Earth is closest to the sun during the winter in the Northern Hemisphere, her speed increases in order to counterbalance the increased strength of the sun's gravity. At the other, distant end of the ellipse, Earth slows down, and summer lingers.

The busy antics of black-capped chickadees are always a cheerful sight in the winter.

In the beginning of the second week of December, 1941, he boarded a bus in Michigan crowded with new recruits and began a four-year journey that saw him make repeated landings in New Guinea and the Philippines. Each time ashore his infantry company of 205 men had the same duty: clear out enemy bunkers, foxholes, and caves so the U.S. could establish a foothold in the territory. It was dangerous work; only 15 were not wounded or killed.

Now, on winter mornings, the old veteran gnarled and stooped with age uses a cane for stability and carries a small can of sunflower seeds over a snow-covered path. At a head-high platform he empties the seeds. Even before he has turned around chickadees are there in force. Through the morning he'll sit with his wife by the woodstove and enjoy the feeder, which has served generation after generation of little birds. More than a half century has washed and bleached the man's memories, leaving only traces of the heavy red stains that once colored everything. Children, grandchildren, and chickadees help him see other things.

They shall not grow old, as we that
*   are left grow old.*
Age shall not weary them, nor the
*   years condemn.*
At the going down of the sun and in
*   the morning*
We will remember them.

—Laurence Binyon
"For the Fallen"
The Times, Sept. 21, 1914

Bobwhite quail need three types of habitat: grassy fields for nesting; weedy fields (or crop fields with waste grain) for winter seeds; and brushy thickets for shelter.

Is it the holidays or is it winter, or is it that powerful combination of winter-holidays that sends us waddling to the gym in January?

Maybe birds can provide a clue. A study of bobwhite quail found food energy requirements for them were lowest in September, and increased by 60 percent in December. Clearly, during cold weather, birds eat more to provide energy to keep warm.

At the same time they gain weight. No surprise there, but weight gain has benefits for them. Greater body weight not only provides additional fat reserves, it also increases thermal efficiency. A larger body has proportionally less heat-radiating surface area than a smaller body, and it has greater thermal inertia. It's axiomatic that for a species with wide distribution, northern individuals are bigger than southern ones.

The average winter weight gain for quail was more than seven percent. For a person weighing 100 lbs., that's a seven pound increase and a notch on the belt. So with the winter holidays, remember: 1) We need more food energy to keep warm; 2) Our bodies try to increase size in order to keep warm; 3) It's hard to resist cookies, pies, and extra helpings.